Love, Colleen
Debbie
Christmas 2012

The Dream Time
The Account of a Ninth Grade Girl of the 60s

The Dream Time
The Account of a Ninth Grade Girl of the 60s
Debbie Bumstead

The Dream Time is a memoir, a work of non-fiction, but I have changed everyone's name but my own in its telling. Cover photos: About 1969, myself at 15 and my childhood home under an early rare fall of snow.

ISBN10: 1480144517

EAN13: 978-1480144514

Printed in the United States of America

For MK, AKA Roberta

Contents

The Dream Time

-One-

My dark heavy shoes clumped on the sidewalk. Everybody looked at me in my old skirt and thought, "What a freak. Her neck sticks out." It was true. I felt pimply and ugly. They all squatted on the curb of the street that bordered the high school, smoking, staring at me as I walked to school. Oh, those almond trees that lined Devonshire street - I looked up into them and through to the sky. The smokers were all older, staring at me every morning, thinking me stupidly square and pure -- looking up into almond leaves! They thought I was a gawk with two club feet. It was a sweetness of lawns and palm trees to pass them, a passing into air that treated me less ugly. Still, I was ugly.

A decade had passed between eighth grade and ninth grade. All the acquaintances of eighth grade had clearer eyes and brighter faces. They had become old friends that I hardly knew. I happily greeted Beth in the algebra class and sat by her. I didn't remember how I knew her before. She greeted me just as pleasantly. The absence over summer brightened us all to each other. My elementary school friend, Jan, who was an enemy in eighth grade, became my best friend in ninth. She and I had our English class together after lunch. We were seated alphabetically, she across the room and I behind another elementary school friend, Suzanne. Suzanne and I greeted each other, and she handed back a folder. The teacher said we were to keep journals in which we wrote for the first five minutes of the period. The teacher was Miss Loch, with long black hair and a tripping up kicky walk. She was the kind of teacher, we thought, that liked the clean quick girls and the impish outspoken boys. The class was full of talk and laughter. I felt dirty and pimply and poorly dressed. I couldn't laugh freely; I couldn't smile without looking at the floor. I never spoke. I thought I was slow and ugly, and I slumped at my desk. Jan did not speak either, but she was neatly dressed and poised. She fell in love with one of the boys in our class.

"Is it Travis?" I asked, because he was the one I liked.

"No," she said.

I thought, and then asked, "Dave?"

"Yes, but you won't tell anyone?"

We talked about Dave. I didn't tell her about Travis. I was embarrassed.

Travis was from Texas and we glanced at each other across the room. He handed out the journal folders and when he came to me, he teased. He let me reach, then pulled the folder away. I laughed and felt self-conscious, but wonderful, and tried again until I had to give up and he put the folder on my desk. He had a wide face and dark eyes. He had a cowboy's swagger and a loud slow drawl. I was embarrassed. I thought everyone had watched, seen me

2

turn red, and then knew that I was in love with the obnoxious fellow who sat over by the bulletin board.

"Can you imagine liking that creep? She is certainly weird," that was what they were saying. But I still thought of him and kept a box of cleaning powder with the brand name, TRAVIS, printed on it in my room at home where I looked at it often, feeling strange and frightened.

In the English class we all spent the first five minutes bent over our journals. I wrote freely and quickly; writing was the action I did without ugliness following. The words were happy or thoughtful, coming sloppily onto the paper, but telling clear. I stared out the window a moment; then I wrote, "I wonder what everybody is thinking in this whole wide world except me..." I drifted into a dream.

Two weeks after the beginning of school Miss Loch collected the journals to read over the weekend. We were eager for praise and success. We looked at all our teachers and asked for compliments. Some of us made jokes and laughed, so appealingly that teachers couldn't help but smile. To us the smile counted for everything. For me it was that way.

On Monday we opened our journals expectantly, hoping for comments. Miss Loch had written me a whole letter. I opened the folder and found it tucked in with my school paper, a sheet of typing paper neatly written on in pencil. She had written me a letter and I read it shyly, with the class growing quiet and far away:

"One of the reasons I so like journals, Debbie, is they give me a chance to see what people like Debbie Bumstead are like underneath the quiet answer-questions-only-if-asked exterior. I think I am going to greatly enjoy reading your journal -- and talking back in roughly the same fashion."

I glanced up at Miss Loch and down again. I wondered if she had watched me read it. I began to feel warm; a lump pressed against my stomach.

"How many points are possible?" asked a boy who had received five points for his journal.

"Ten," Miss Loch replied.

"Did anyone get ten?" someone asked.

"Yes," she answered, "one person got fifteen." She looked at me and away. I felt hot and red and full of love. It was I who received fifteen out of ten points for my journal and a letter, too. I loved Miss Loch.

****

In the early morning algebra class we all sat in our desks, stiff with worry and concentration. If I lost the thread, or misunderstood the step, they would go ahead until I was far far behind. So I sat up straight. I didn't dream. My stomach felt full of fear, but I didn't get lost. Those who had, slouched in their seats and came in after school for tutoring. But I was successful in a timid way and I became fond of Mr. Wharton, the algebra teacher.

But it was Mr. Bayard I wanted to marry.

I walked across the grass to the Art building after Algebra. Mr. Bayard leaned against the open door. He was short and pudgy with a voice that came through his nose, but he was romantic in a lonely suffering way. He was like us, the fourteen year olds with pimples, though he was twenty-five and had no skin problems. He was a teenager grown older and wiser and lonelier. He looked like a poet to me, leaning there against the old peeling-paint building. He lifted a hand in salute while I was still across the lawn. It was easy to smile back at him. He watched me walk toward him and I was not afraid of what he saw.

"He·low, Deb-o-rah," he said everyday.

I sat with five other girls at a group of tables. Two of the girls were seniors who seemed tall and elegant to me. I thought that when I was a senior I wouldn't look like that, but my friend, Jan, would. She dressed well and stood straight, like Lisa and Susan. I stood stoop-shouldered. My clothes were either old or too large. It didn't matter in Mr. Bayard's class.

We got out our ink bottles and pens and brushes to continue work on our drawings. The whole class was talking and happy as we worked. I looked over at Mr. Bayard. He sat alone at another group of desks, his chin in his hands, staring out the open door. He was looking into the green grass and dreaming. I rested my eyes on him, seeing his curly blue-black hair and dark eyes. He had an olive complexion. I was dreaming, too.

"Oh, darn!" Susan exclaimed. She had made a black blot in the middle of her street scene. Mr. Bayard got up and came over. We all expressed sympathy. Susan was angry with herself. She said, "Well, that's that, I'll have to throw it away."

"No ," I said suddenly, "you can always make that blot into something." I smiled at her. Mr. Bayard was looking at me.

He said, "That's true. Work it into the picture." Mr. Bayard looked at me.

I dreamed that Mr. Bayard lived in a little wooden house on the other side of State street. I dreamed that I lived there also. At night in bed before I went to sleep that is what I dreamed. That Mr. Bayard and I loved each other with sweetness and romantic sorrow. That in the evenings we sat close to each other on the couch in a late sunny golden room in his house. That in the mornings we walked to school, going down the main street of town, looking in store windows and talking, turning down through the park. That we held hands in the park, looking up, not into almond leaves, but pine boughs and oak. And we were so in love.

I dreamed that the whole school was in a tizzy over us, but we ignored it. I dreamed that we went to school as usual, I as a student and he as an art teacher, that through the day we each knew who loved us - he loved me and I loved him. But my dream had a melancholy haze through it, as if our love were a gold twilight. Sometimes I ended up crying a little, thinking of his dark eyes and appealing nature, of us living together, sinking into a sad honey-liquid love. Then I fell asleep, finally, curled into a night of sweet tears and sad romance.

****

In November it began to rain every day. During September Jan and I ate lunch beside a cluster of three small palm trees, sitting there with our legs folded under our skirts, talking with laughter and joy. We made up stories about strange people and lands on different planets. We liked to tell stories. My mind felt full of color and fun; I went on eagerly and we put our heads back to laugh. Sometimes Jan came up with an idea which I considered pure genius. I marveled at the idea. I saw the earth from another planet. It rolled, a round ball, in space, everything that lived there distant from me, and complete, a full egg

6

held in an empty space.

The high school was like a small world floating in its own space. In November when it began to rain Jan and I wandered around and around the science building, under the shelter of the eaves, eating as we walked and watching the gray rain fall. We didn't tell pretend stories; we spoke of the people we passed; we talked about their places and ours in this little planet of school.

Jan wanted to belong to the group of football players and their girlfriends. These girls all dressed in beautiful store bought clothes - a soft coral sweater with a matching skirt, or a light blue and tan striped outfit. I liked to see the colors they wore and their gleaming full and bouncing hair; they were perfectly groomed. The football crowd was the popular one. They stood under the tin roofs beside the old lockers, gathered in loud circles facing inward. They were all upper classmen.

We freshmen were still new. We were only beginning to ease into our particular groups. Some of us would belong to the popular football set; some of us would wander longingly along the out-skirts of it. Some would become the smokers who sat along Devonshire street to puff on their cigarettes. Some of us would belong to small groups of four or five - girls who were never asked out on dates, boys who spent the lunch hour horsing around the library. And when we had entered our particular group, we belonged; we had a home in our little world. Only certain individuals did not belong to any class, but were accepted by all or none. I didn't think I would be that kind of person, but I wasn't easing toward any group. I could have belonged to the intellectuals, but I didn't try hard enough. I could belong to the group of girls who didn't get dates, but I didn't care enough about having a boyfriend. I could belong to the group that wandered around the popular ones, but I didn't care enough about that either. If there was any group I should have belonged to, it would have been a group that loved their teachers.

I always looked forward to the lunch hour when Jan and I walked around the science building. I hoped that we would pass some of my teachers and they would say hello to me. We walked along, commenting on how lucky it was that the rain had let up for the ball game that night and I saw out of the corner of my eye Mr. Neil, my science teacher, opening the door of his room. We passed and he said, "Hi, Debbie." I was pleased and full of a secret happiness.

We walked on and I peeled my orange. As we went around the end of the building and up again I saw Miss Loch coming toward us. I had begun to think I walked like her, scuffing my heels jauntily and stepping out quickly. She wore a poplin raincoat that I thought was incredibly perfect for her. I wanted one like it, though I knew it wouldn't look good on me. It was striped horizontally in muted black and white. The stripes faded into each other and Miss Loch's black hair fell down her back. I bit into my orange self-consciously as we neared her.

She said, "Hello, ladies!" I smiled shyly into my orange and Jan said hello. When Miss Loch was almost at the end of the building she turned and called, "Debbie Bumstead, you..." But though we turned to hear I was so nervous my ears rang. I smiled and raised my hand in acknowledgment and we turned again to continue walking.

"What did she mean by that?" Jan asked.

"I didn't hear what she said," I said.

The Dream Time

"She said, 'Debbie Bumstead, you don't like to be called a lady, do you?'"

Jan and I looked at each other in puzzlement. I considered for a long time, but still couldn't figure out what Miss Loch meant. I thought, I don't mind being called a lady. How did I act to make her say that? I thought maybe it was my clothes, my old homemade corduroy skirt and my funny gray vinyl coat. But then I thought, she wouldn't say that because of my ugly clothes; it must be something else. But I never figured it out, although I thought about it for weeks afterward.

Jan and I walked to my house after school. My house had a basement and that was where Jan and I liked to talk and play. We went through boxes of old clothes and found some dolls, Barbie, Ken, Midge, and Andy, along with doll clothes which my mother had made for them. We cleared off a trunk lid to make the dolls a house. Barbie and Midge lived in the house. Ken and Andy came to the house to ask the girls to a formal dance. So we dressed the dolls and undressed them, seeing which outfit was the right thing for them to wear. That was the way we played, by dressing the dolls for different occasions. We couldn't pretend as well as we did in elementary school. Now we just dressed them and told stories and felt a little self-conscious. Still our play also made us feel young and happy. When we finished we made our cots up - after the football game Jan was spending the night and we were going to sleep in the basement - and I found a half-size blanket that I used as a cape as we flew up the stairs and out the trapdoor. I whirled into the living room like a fearsome doom-calling crow, surprising my family members, and Jan and I laughed self-consciously.

Debbie Bumstead

We wore our jeans and thick coats to the football game. It was a clear cold night after a week of rain and everyone was starry-eyed and dark-haired. I felt beautiful in the cold night; my smile wanted to blossom; my ears wanted to wiggle with joy! Everyone else was just as happy and active; we walked back and forth to the snack bar; we sat in the stands and stamped our feet; we looked around at people we knew; we felt like we knew everyone and were friends with everyone. Sometimes we rested our dancing eyes on the distant buzz of color in the field and stood to yell when there was a touchdown. But mostly it was sitting close and cold, listening to the cheerleaders and the band, and noticing, suddenly, the great clouds of moths around the tall lamps.

I looked down the rows of seated fans and saw Miss Loch walking on the ground in a crowd of milling people. She had her hair in a bun. Jan said she didn't like Miss Loch's hair that way. I thought it only made her more strange and lovely to me. I watched her. She looked up into the stands, but didn't see me. When people who knew her stopped to speak, she acted interested. She looked at them in the studious penetrating way she looked at me sometimes and I was jealous and lonely. I wanted her to be only interested in me.

Now the night acquired a gauze of thoughtfulness and longing. It was quieter, a silence had pushed everyone behind a curtain except Miss Loch and me. My eyes were still full of stars, lonely stars. The core that threw out the curtain rested in the pit of my stomach and the curtain was a drape of dream. "Miss Loch, be mine," I said inside myself. I wanted to be hers.

The Dream Time

****

Another clear night shone down as my father and I stepped across the campus grass. It was Back-to-School night when our parents could go through a miniature version of our day at school. My mother decided not to go. It was just my father and I. I thought my father was handsome, and I liked people to see us together. They would think, "That is Debbie's dad. He looks like a hippy. He's really with it. She must be, too." From my father they would see that I was not square and dull. They would say, "Her father's an artist. She must be an artist, too."

After ten minutes of Algebra, we walked to the Art building. Mr. Bayard stood at his door, greeting some parents. When we came up, he smiled. "He—low, Deb—o —rah."

"Hi. This is my father," I began to introduce them, but I was awkward. They introduced themselves. "Max Bumstead," my father said. "Gene Bayard," Mr. Bayard said, and they shook hands. I thought a strange ceremony had been performed. Someone from my regular everyday life had shaken hands with someone I was secretly, passionately, in love with. My father didn't know and Mr. Bayard didn't know of the secret strangeness of what had just happened. They went on into the room and Mr. Bayard pointed out a large pencil still-life I did that won an honorable mention at the county contest. It was on the wall with a small pen and ink drawing of a castle I had made up.

My father nodded at the still-life when Mr. Bayard said, "It won an award!" I wondered if Mr. Bayard was proud of me or if he wanted my father to be proud. My father said he liked the castle better, because it was more creative. We all laughed and I agreed. Then Mr. Bayard moved off to the other parents.

I pointed out another picture of mine up on the opposite wall. It was a green monochrome painting of several snakes twined in and out of one another. Each snake had a different pattern on its skin. It was not a significant picture in itself, but because of the event it stirred, I thought it might be a symbol of Mr. Bayard's and my secret relationship. I had worked on it for a week or so. It required a lot of easy yet meticulous painting. One day I finished the snakes and planned to go on and paint in a background. But that night I had a bad dream. I dreamed I was trapped in a car with an octopus that had weaving venomous snakes for tentacles. It chased me around the car, wiggling and hissing until my heart hurt with the fright of it. Finally I pinned the beast down with my foot and squished it; the guts popped and I woke up hot and scared.

Then I decided I wouldn't touch that painting again. But the next day I found it staring down at me from the wall. Mr. Bayard thought it didn't need a background and he had tacked it up, right after my horrible dream. I felt like he knew. I suddenly felt like he knew everything, that I loved him, that I thought of him all the time; I felt like he knew my daydreams. He knew everything after all, but never spoke of it and I never spoke of it. But he knew I had a crush on him. It stayed secret and only came out a little on certain occasions and sometimes when we looked at each other.

My father and I walked over to the old main building to visit my geography class. Geography was the only class I disliked. The teacher was the sort of person who didn't remember anyone's name. I did not like that at all. I was afraid of being a nobody. People looked at my face and tried to remember my name. Betty? Suzy? They thought I had a common name. But my name was Mary Deborah Alice Bumstead and even to be called Debbie Bumstead was not common. They didn't remember in Geography.

When my father and I had been for ten minutes in each of my classrooms, we wandered home. We spoke a little about Geography. "Doesn't she act funny?" I said of my teacher, because of the way she smiled as she walked and didn't look at anyone.

"She is self-conscious," my father said.

That was a revelation to me. I saw that it was true. She was self-conscious, perhaps because of her chest which stuck out formidably and made a shelf for her head to rest on. Now I felt some compassion for her. I, also, was self-conscious - because of my pimples, my long neck, my old clothes, and my posture. I knew that I was gawky and unattractive.

My father was quiet. I sighed with my thoughts.

"I really liked your art teacher," my father said, "He seemed open and ready for new ideas."

I agreed, and thought my secret thoughts. My father and I walked home in the night.

****

It began to rain again. The grass became a swamp. Puddles formed on the sidewalks and filled with worms that died and left an incredible stink. People ran from one building to the next, getting to their classes early and

13

chattering happily there. The teachers had problems quieting us. I wrote in my English journal that even though people didn't like the rain it made them smile more; it made them more friendly. Mr. Bayard brought in a record player so that we could listen to music as we worked. We had only two records. One was by the Doors. When the singer sang in his deep close voice about slipping into unconsciousness, a daydream began to revolve around the song and the rain. I dreamed that after school I was in the art room. I stood on a ladder to tack up pictures. Mr. Bayard was in the clean-up room. He wanted to make love to me. He could hardly contain himself. The dream was so exciting my heart began to pound. He came into the big room. I was startled and my foot slipped. I fell to the floor. I slipped into unconsciousness. Mr. Bayard could no longer hold back. He made love to me.

I dreamed that dream right in the classroom! Mr. Bayard was standing at his podium, staring out into the rain and I had been there dreaming that fantasy. I was embarrassed. I still had the fear from my childhood that some people could read my mind and listen in on all my shocking daydreams.

But I couldn't stop. I dreamed that I had Mr. Bayard's baby. It was a boy with curly black hair and dark blue eyes. His name was Nathan. Now he was two years old. He wore a little striped tee-shirt and blue shorts with tennis shoes. It was a sunny day and the boy and I walked down the street. He had brown skin and a lot of hair. He was beautiful.

I looked up again at Mr. Bayard. I saw that he was dreaming, too. And I dreamed that he was dreaming of me.

The Dream Time

It rained so steadily that it became a rhythm that we lived to. It was a running beat; we lived and dreamed as if we were galloping steadily, steadily. We got up, went to school, changed classes at the same time each day; we smiled, dreamed, talked, all to the beat of the rain, until we were beating, too, and could fall like raindrops into sleep if we weren't so full of excitement and rain-joy. I heard Miss Loch say, " Lub-dub," to Miss Richter, the team teacher. I learned that those were the words to describe the sound of a beating heart. "Lub—dub," I thought, "Lub-dub."

But it was a popular song on the radio that became a symbol for the rain and my dreams and the excitement of living I felt during my ninth grade school year. The cafeteria played the radio everyday, and Jan and I had begun to go to the cafeteria to buy desserts. The popular song was a silly one called, *Dizzy*. I stood and waited for Jan at the door. Almost everyday I heard it, about being dizzy, head spinning like a whirlpool. Years afterward when I chanced to hear the song, I was overcome with a strangely painful nostalgia. If anyone wondered when that song came out, I could tell them instantly, "It was 1969." The year of rain and love.

When Jan and I were walking around the science building she told me that yesterday at brunch, the ten minutes we had between first and second periods, she was running from the cafeteria to the office when Miss Loch offered to share her umbrella, since they were both going in the same direction. I wished that it had been me walking with Miss Loch. I wished I could have been there. Jan liked Miss Loch, too. She told me that she thought she would begin starting her name with a "J " that looked like Miss Loch's "J's." I agreed that they were nice. Jan liked

Debbie Bumstead

Miss Loch, but I loved her. Miss Loch liked Jan, but she thought I was special. Miss Loch thought I was special, but sometimes I wondered if she liked me.

And in the rain my mother and father gave me a puppy. I named him Peter. He was small and black, tan, and white. On Saturday I sat on the old couch on the back porch with Pete lying beside me. He was mine to take care of. When the rain stopped I would take him for walks and teach him to come when I called. I rested my head on his back, but I dreamed my Saturdays were spent in a different way.

I dreamed that I was a spy and had been told to watch Miss Loch. I had a briefcase in which I kept maps and notes. I wore special spying clothes: jeans and tennis shoes, so that whoever saw me would think I was just a kid playing around. On a sunny Saturday I sighed and said, "Well, off to work," and I walked to Miss Loch's house. In real life I didn't know where it was or what it looked like, though I knew she lived in the country and had a horse. I had to imagine her house. I dreamed that it was on a corner set up on a grassy knoll. Around the yard was a short brick wall with bushes growing near it. I climbed onto the wall and peered through the bushes. In a business-like way I opened my briefcase and took notes, describing the place and noting down the color of the horse and the dog in the backyard. Miss Loch then came out of the house, got into her car and drove away.

I dashed to the porch of her house and slipped indoors. The house was full of daylight and cheerfulness. I went through, taking note of everything. I sorted through her papers carefully. I looked into her refrigerator. I studied everything until I had a fine objective description of Miss

Loch's surroundings. Now I could report in and the dream drifted to an end. In a sudden clear thought I visualized one part of my mind as the organization that had asked me to spy on Miss Loch. Now it would use my studies to make me resemble her. That was what I wanted.

****

Mr. Bayard gave us an art project called scratchboard drawing. We painted a piece of colored cardboard over with black acrylic and then scratched out a picture with a pin, so the drawing lines were red or blue or yellow with a black background. We were all ready to begin scratching. Lisa was sitting next to me and she raised her hand. She was smiling so I knew she was going to tease. She teased Mr. Bayard as if he were younger than she. He seemed vulnerable, like a child, to Lisa, so he could be teased. I laughed, watching. My mouth got ready and my eyes filled with pleasure. Mr. Bayard came over. He knew, too, that we were going to play. His mouth twitched, also, and I saw that he liked us.

"Yes, Lisa," he said.

Lisa pouted, "What am I going to draw?"

Mr. Bayard sighed. He looked at both Lisa and me. I saw that I was going to be an accomplice. He pointed at the black piece of cardboard and asked me, "What color is this?" meaning what color was under the black.

But I teased him. I bent over and said, "It looks like black to me."

It was so simple. Everyone at the table laughed. Mr. Bayard snorted, "Debbie!" and then ruffled my hair. He put his hand on my head and ruffled my short hair. My hair was

Debbie Bumstead

short and clean and his hand rested there and playfully ruffled it. We all laughed. They all wanted their hair to be ruffled, but it was I, and they all knew Mr. Bayard liked me and I knew Mr. Bayard liked me. It was perfect. But then in English I was assigned to hand out journal folders. I didn't like to. We came into class and sat down. Miss Loch asked us to be quiet while she took roll. Then while everyone was quiet and not doing anything, I had to get up, fumble with the filing cabinet, and begin to hand out the folders. The whole class watched me and saw how my neck stuck out and my shoulders drooped. They were repulsed by my pimples. I walked across the front to give Miss Richter's portion of the class their folders. Everyone was watching, even Miss Loch. She stood at the podium and watched me walk toward her. Her eyes stared. They penetrated. I felt color rising in my face. She looked at me as if she were studying me for a report on my behavior. I glanced at her and she smiled.

She said, "That's a very pretty sweater, Debbie."

I smiled down at my feet. My sweater was thin, pink, and soft, and very old, a hand-me-down.

After we had written in our journals and the person who had to pick them up had done so, we got into separate groups. We were going to put on plays. The assignment was to put a TV show into the setting of a fairy tale. Our group had Star Trek to be set to The Three Billy Goats Gruff. Suzanne was in my group. Travis wasn't. I saw that Travis was in a group that gathered around where I usually sat. He was sitting in my usual desk. I watched him. He laughed and talked loudly in his Texan accent.

I was unsure of why I liked him. But he looked at me often with his deep-set brown eyes. We had never

The Dream Time

spoken to each other. When we all went back to our seats I sat where he had been sitting and the seat was hot. The seat was warm and the warmth went into my body. I felt like I was touching him. The heat of his body moved into mine. I became flushed and could hardly sit still. There in the public classroom with all the students chattering around me I felt that private and sexual desire rising in me. I looked over at Travis. He was sitting quietly and not looking at me.

It was time for our plays. Suzanne and I changed into pants in the restroom. I was different in pants. I was more sure of my movements. I felt natural and true. I wore light blue jeans and my pink sweater and could have jumped with happiness. I was not scared! It didn't worry me to be in front of the class with my friends in jeans, saying our lines clearly, cleverly. I noticed Miss Loch watching. The class laughed and we were full of the joy of our accomplishment and comradeship. Travis was laughing. I looked over at Jan. Her group was next. Miss Loch bored into me with her eyes. She thought I was special.

I had Physical Education after English. When it wasn't raining we went out to play a soggy form of softball. We played cautiously, so that we wouldn't slip in the mud. I was a fair player. I always hit grounders down the line to the shortstop. In the field I was better, but I wasn't a favorite with my team-mates. They thought I was ugly and unpopular, so they put me in the outfield. They didn't give me a mitt. I stood out there looking in. It was a strange sight - the girls standing in their places while the world froze around them. I was on the outside, watching. Then a senior on the other team hit a fly ball. It came to me. I caught it with bare hands against my chest.

Mrs. White was watching. She said, "You sure aren't

19

afraid of the ball, are you?" I smiled. My left breast was throbbing with pain.

On the way back to the locker room I carried the bats. I walked with Miss Montgomery. Miss Montgomery was a quiet person. The girls called her, "Monty" and Mrs. White, just "White," but I didn't. I called them Miss Montgomery and Mrs. White. They called me "Bumstead."

Miss Montgomery told me about her plans for the weekend. She said, "I am going to the desert. Have you ever been to Joshua Tree Monument?"

"No," I said, shyly.

In the locker room all of us had to take showers. We pulled off our neat white P.E. clothes and walked into the showers. If the water was cold we danced around quickly and jumped out; if it was hot we stayed under and closed our eyes because it felt so good. My left breast was red where the ball had hit it. I covered myself with a towel. It was weird, I thought, to be in a large building, naked, with forty other naked girls. I was used to being naked only in the bathroom at home. Here the space was as large as two classrooms and we were wandering about it naked. I thought it was very strange. One of the girls in my locker row weighed 200 pounds. I looked at her fat buttocks. Another girl was slender with smooth olive-tinted skin. She was pregnant. She was slender and young like I was, but she was pregnant. A small round ball rested inside and made her belly protrude a little. I thought she was beautiful.

We dressed and went outside to wait for the bell to ring. I stood on the basketball courts with a couple of other girls. Miss Montgomery came over and asked us, "Do you know the time?"

I didn't have a watch, but I lifted my right arm and

looked at my wrist. I said, "I guess I don't have a watch."
"That's the wrong wrist," Miss Montgomery said. I looked at my left wrist and there wasn't a watch there, either. Miss Montgomery said, "You are kind of dumb, aren't you, Bumstead?"
The other girls and I laughed. I felt pleased and dumb.
At home I looked at myself in the bathroom mirror. I looked at my sweater to see what Miss Loch saw. It was a delicate sweater with sleeves a little short, so that my wrists, which Miss Montgomery saw, were revealed. My shoulders were sharp and my breasts small. In the dim light of the bathroom I thought I looked pensive and sorrowful. My eyes seemed dark and full of questions. I smiled. My smile was beautiful in a sad way, I thought. I put my hand on my head to ruffle my hair and feel what Mr. Bayard felt. I leaned on the sink and stared into my eyes. I wondered who I really was.
I fell into a quiet mood. In my bedroom I played records. Simon and Garfunkel's voices were soft like silk, like gentleness, as they sang of the moon rising over a field and how empty and aching they were.
I felt it was true. I felt it in me. I ached and I didn't know why. My chest felt empty and hurting. I was as sad as I was full of love. I thought the world was like a teardrop crying for the beauty of living. I wanted to be loved. I wanted to be loved.

****

On the last day before Christmas vacation it snowed. It got so cold that it snowed in Hemet. It made us jump and laugh. Out on the lawn we lifted our hands and put back our heads; it was snowing in Hemet! School let out early and I walked home slowly, looking up into the falling snow. I saw each flake come into focus out of the white sky, drifting down; I thought the flakes were winter moths dancing happy in the cold air. I was happy, too. I thought of my last class of the day, Life Science, with Mr. Neil. It was the only class that I went to eagerly for learning - learning the science of our life, of our bodies and minds.

I also liked Mr. Neil. When the class laughed at something funny he always looked at me to share a smile. He had a quizzical smile. At the end of class he had called me up to his desk. He told me I was earning "A's" too easily, that I should be in the biology class. He called me an under-achiever. I was wearing a black sweater and he looked at it and then into my face. I didn't know what to say. It was snowing and we both laughed suddenly and I said good-bye.

The next day the snow was gone and the long Christmas vacation began. I walked with Pete, my little dog, over to the high school campus each day. He ran happily in the dying grass and I wandered, with my hands in my pockets, along the walkways and out into the square where the cheerleaders had yelled and danced. I remembered the days that had passed. I thought of Miss Loch and Mr. Bayard and I said to myself that I loved them and that I wanted to be near them for always. I dreamed of being cuddled close to them. It felt sweet to dream of it there in the cold clear lonely day.

But even as I dreamed, at the edge of my sight there was a disturbing movement over on the grass, and I heard a squeal of laughter. I glanced at Pete and saw that he stood with his ears cocked. I felt an ugliness rising in my stomach. I didn't want to see it. Why was it so ugly? They were jerking and pumping, right there on the withered grass of the high school. The girl was wearing pink pants. Her legs were flapping in the air. The boy was wearing jeans, banging against her. Oh, it was ugly. I felt hot and sick. For an instant I wondered if the girl had a hole in her pants, but then it was too awful and I wanted to run. I called Pete and we walked away quickly.

That's what it looked like. That's what it looked like when two people made love to each other; I didn't want to call it love anymore. I felt so sick that I began to sweat in the cold air. But two bodies were made to fit that way; good and beautiful babies came that way. That's the way it happened. I couldn't think; I was sick. Why was making love so disturbing for my heart to see? I didn't want to call it love anymore. Pete and I ran down the sidewalk, letting the cold air rush in to clean it all away.

We stopped at the entrance to the alley. I stared at the ground, breathless, and suddenly felt like crying. I didn't know what to make of it. I wanted to dissolve into the air; I wanted to feel straight and dark like the trees. I wanted the snow to come back and I wanted to lie like cold silence as snow over the earth, as clean quiet snow over the land. I wanted to cover my eyes; I wanted to cover my ears; I wanted to be clean snow covering the land.

Debbie Bumstead

-Two-

School began again with clear frosty days. In the mornings I found myself curled into a tight ball to keep warm. I woke to vague memories of night dreams or thoughts on philosophical questions - I did not move for a moment, wondering, strangely, about stones and whether there were souls living in them. My mother called the time to me and I stretched. I dressed quickly in the cold morning, moving so eagerly and so full of anticipation that sometimes a gasp of excitement escaped from me.

In the bathroom I splashed my face with icy water and exclaimed, "Oh!" It was another day of school and dreaming and possibilities. I was eager to be off, down the winter alleyway and along Devonshire, looking always up into almond trees and feeling self-conscious under the stares of the students who sat on the curb smoking. I still felt ugly, but now I was eager. Even if none of the possibilities

The Dream Time

occurred, my regular schedule would allow me some joy. I would at least be able to listen to my teachers.

Some days we students were full of smiles and happy chatter. We listened to lectures and helped make the room laugh with the goodness of living. Some days we were tired and irritated with school. We did not cooperate; we sat sullenly and didn't care what we heard. This day I fell into a pensive mood. All the previous week I had been looking in books and magazines for poems to complete an assignment in English. The reading of them had made me become thoughtful.

Quietly I watched my algebra teacher. I glanced over at Travis and rested my eyes on him a moment. I felt separated from the class. I felt as if I were watching them through a window. When the bell rang I got up slowly. Travis was in a hurry and bumped into me. He turned and said, teasing, "Better watch where you're going." He looked at me and I smiled. But inside I was so full of quietness that I didn't feel flustered. I smiled and glanced into his dark eyes. Inside I was calm and quiet. It was the first time he had ever spoken to me, but I didn't seem to notice.

The students stood by their lockers during the ten minute brunch period. I walked through them, with my notebook resting on my hip, and listened to the waves of noise rushing in the cold air. I looked at individual people quietly, watching them without thinking. My mind was quiet inside. Usually I talked to myself about everything I saw. Not today. My mouth was still and quiet. Jan joined me and we stepped through the crowd, dodging carefully, not stopping until we were on the edge of the lawn in front of the Art building. I looked across at the old vanilla-colored building. Mr. Bayard was inside.

Debbie Bumstead

Why was it, we all wondered, that love was important? We were even unsure of what it meant. We thought love was kissing and going to the movies together and feeling each other's bodies. An excitement entered our stomachs and chests and we said it was love. A dark drape hung in back and when a breeze lifted it an inch, a bright light flashed out into the blackness. Then we were suddenly unsure of our definitions. They were all ugly to me now. I began to think love was more dreaming than touching.

Jan told me of her wishes. She dreamed that Dave was her boyfriend. She watched him; every movement and word was important. I began to think that she loved him more than Linda did and Linda was his girlfriend and could touch him physically. I wondered, is love only a sweet dream? Love is dream, I said to myself, dreaming is loving.

The bell for class rang. Jan left and I wandered slowly across the lawn. I paused an instant in the doorway. Mr. Bayard looked at me and said, "He-low, Deb-o-rah." I smiled. The class gathered and we worked on our drawings. I was still quiet, so quiet that it affected my hand. I doodled lightly. I rested my head down on my other arm and doodled some lines of words. It was an awkward poem. I was not thinking about anything, but the words fell out quietly - questions on the sincerity of gestures of affection. I felt tired and sleepy. I closed my eyes.

I heard Mr. Bayard coming over. I opened my eyes and covered the poem with my hand. Mr. Bayard stopped behind me. He took his hand and lifted mine up by the wrist, his big hand and my thin wrist, and read my poem. I was still resting my head on the desk and as he read I felt my face growing hot. Hot liquid gathered in my stomach. I felt faint. Mr. Bayard was reading my awkward questions on love; he was reading me. The whole world grew absolutely still and silent.

When he finished he laid my wrist down gently and walked away. He worked in the corner straightening papers, with his back to me. He was embarrassed and I was, also. Would he think the poem was about him? My stomach was in a turmoil and I wanted to cry; tears gathered in my eyes; my fists clinched. I felt like Mr. Bayard took his hand and opened a window and a whole flood of myself flowed in to him. He went below the surface. Right there in the real world where we lived together and with everyone else he held my wrist and knew just me behind the curtains. It was frightening and embarrassing; I felt like he had trespassed my private property. At the same time I felt such pain that it was beautiful. Oh, love. I wanted to cry.

At lunch I sat with Jan and a few other girls in the cafeteria. Jan and Beth were talking excitedly about something. I only heard the rhythm of their chatter against the roar of the rest of the cafeteria. I couldn't quite think of what had happened to me. Slowly I chewed on a sandwich and sipped at my milk. It was a clear cold day in winter and I felt like my heart was outside me, revealed, in the crisp naked air.

What of love then? I wondered. I stared down the row of tables and my thoughts revolved silently. The whole cafeteria was full of people who were thinking of love. But I was not going to think of it that way anymore. Now love was dream.

Jan and I walked across the campus to our English class. We had been working busily all month on ditto sheets. While everyone was working, the teachers passed back the notebooks in which we had put the collections of poems we liked. Miss Loch handed me mine and I opened it to see my grade. It was 60/60 and there was a note underneath -- "I always enjoy getting a chance to see into your mind a little - you are a very interesting young lady. Thank you for giving me beautiful and fun poems to read."

I smiled to myself. I looked up to find Miss Loch. She stood at the front of the room looking at me. She had watched me read her comment. Her eyes were hard and searching. I smiled at her. Her face broke into a smile, too, and we smiled across the busy heads, smiling our understanding. But her eyes were still hard; she stared too long, smiling, and I felt myself growing red. I glanced down shyly and couldn't look up again. Out of the corner of my eye I saw she hadn't moved. She was still studying me, while I turned hot and red.

Oh, what a day, I thought. The rest of my classes went in a spin; Art and English were like rooms occupying my heart. In the rooms Mr. Bayard and Miss Loch wandered and smiled, looking out the windows into me, and my heart loved what was in it.

In the evening I sat in my bedroom thinking of what had happened. I imagined Mr. Bayard, right at that moment, sitting in a chair quietly, thinking of what he had read of mine. Perhaps he wondered if the poem was to him from me and he felt a lump in his stomach, just as a lump rested in mine. I sat on the floor by the record player, looking down at my arm, the one he had picked up. My wrist burned. I wondered if Mr. Bayard's fingers were burning. I started to cry. I was lonely in the night, still unsure of everything. I played record after record, the music drifted...and a daydream filtered through...

A mansion stands in the center of many gardens... a

rose garden, a grove of trees, a fruit orchard surrounded by an old stone wall, a vegetable garden, and jungles of trees and flowers together, run through with winding paths. Beyond the gardens deep forests and rounding grass hills stretched forever, leaving the mansion isolated in a land of magic and dream. This is the place we come to... Mr. Bayard, Miss Loch, and I, and the rest of the teachers I like and Jan and Travis and Dave.

We start up the elegant marble stairs to the front entrance of the mansion. Some of us speak to another, about how we came to be here. We wander into the hallway and separate into drifting pairs and singles. Alone, I enter a front room where many paned windows reach from floor to ceiling and throw sunlight onto the thick rose-colored carpet. When I stand in the sunlight I am warmed. I step through a dining room into a large tiled kitchen with a fireplace, a breakfast table, and full of the smell of fresh bread. I see Miss Loch looking out the kitchen door.

"Hello, Debbie," she says, smiling, "I see a stable down there." We walk together. Music plays magically into the air, as if it were the air.

> *"Are you going to Scarborough Fair?*
> *Parsley, Sage, Rosemary, and Thyme,*
> *Remember me to the one who lives there,*
> *She once was a true love of mine..."*

I walk with Miss Loch past vegetable gardens...under trees that sift the sun down to us...over grass thick and dark like the carpets in the mansion. We come to the stables. Every horse is dancing, groomed, dark-eyed...there are twenty, Arabians, jumpers, pintos, and Morgans. Nearby in a kennel there are Great Danes, Salukis, collies, German shepherds. Miss Loch and I wander together, close and friendly; the music drifts...

> *Alone, I explore the forested grounds. A deer bounds past me. The trees reach up from the flowered earth and I tap happily from one path stone to the next. I thump over a wooden bridge. The path curves round a pond of lily pads and goldfish. Mr. Bayard sits on a stone bench and I sit with him. Flowers grow up around the bench...*

> *"I could almost see a unicorn here," I say. The music plays...*

> *It is the song,* Wanderlove, *and when Mason Williams sings of wandering with his love through life, I dream Mr. Bayard and I wander in life together, too. We watch the seasons go by; we find out how things happen and how they pass. We cross the tall mountains and we ride the waves at sea. And at the end of the song, we are the two who live for each other, Mr. Bayard for me, and I for him. As we listen to the song, looking across the shimmering pond, we smile with friendship.*

> *We all gather in the dining room for supper. The sun sends a glow through the window onto the heavy wood furniture and china dishes. I sit across from Miss Loch and Mr. Bayard; next to me sits Jan and Mr. Neil; Mr. Wharton, Mrs. White, Miss Montgomery, Travis and Dave are there, too. We are all happy and talkative.*

> *Mr. Bayard and Miss Loch watch me as we listen to the music. It's* The Dangling Conversation, *sung by Simon and Garfunkel, about an afternoon with the sun slanting in through the curtains and making shadows in the room. At the words I glance at the windows and around the room. Miss Loch and Mr. Bayard smile.*

The Dream Time

When the lyrics tell of a serious and sad sort of scene, I make fun of the mood. I take a drink of my milk and cross my eyes over the glass. Mr. Bayard and Miss Loch burst out laughing. And then, as the song sifts away on soft voices, I sigh, falling into a thoughtful mood, and I smile, a little sadly, across at Miss Loch and Mr. Bayard. They smile quietly back.

All of our bedrooms are up the carpeted stairs in rooms rich and huge with half-circle windows and window-seats, satin-covered four-poster beds, famous paintings on the walls, and closets of beautiful clothes. I dress in a luscious velvet nightgown and robe. Jan comes in. She is dressed in green and I am in blue. We sit on the bed talking.

"Dave and I were in one of the rooms together this afternoon and we talked awhile," she says. I tell her Travis and I have plans to ride horses together. We laugh with pleasure. It is beautiful and rich here, the gardens grow loveliness, and we own dancing animals to ride over the far hills and forests. We live in a land where only we exist, no other humans, no cities, no ugliness. We will live here forever, free - with only magic to help us, magic and dream.

Jan goes to her bedroom. I walk alone down the hall, my bare feet sinking into the carpet. I open Mr. Bayard's bedroom door. It is dark. He is in bed and I get into bed with him. We do not speak. We sleep together like children, like friends, there is no ugliness in this dreamland. I sleep warmly, safely, full of peace, and Mr. Bayard sleeps beside me. In the morning he wakes and looks down on me. The morning sunlight flows in at the windows and falls on me softly. The music begins again, For Emily, the prettiest song I know, and Mr. Bayard is singing it to me in Garfunkel's voice. I am the dreamer in the song, and I with my hair spread on the pillow, I am the girl that runs through the night, and walks with him in a frosty field under the lamp's light. I am the one he holds hands with, and I am the one he kisses gently, and when he sings, "Oh, I love you, girl," I am the girl he loves.

The Dream Time

-Three-

I n the late spring the trees were almost full with summer. Each day after school I went back to the campus with Pete. I found a discarded tennis racquet and began to practice batting a ball against the backboard. Afterward we wandered across the grass. We decided to walk home the back way and as Pete and I neared the basketball courts I saw Mr. Bayard shooting baskets with another art teacher. As I passed, Mr. Bayard and I smiled. It was too far away for us to speak, but he raised his hand and I saluted him back. Even over the distance I could see him gazing at me with his mouth in a crooked little smile. It was the smile he had that asked me a question and I didn't know what the question was and I didn't know how to answer.

Debbie Bumstead

In the easy spring days I had been dreaming that Mr. Bayard was my friend and we did things together. I dreamed that on Saturdays we walked around town. We went to the library together and looked for good books. We sat across from each other at the big oak library tables, whispering. We bought lunch at the A&W and took the food to the park. We ate there and talked. We became best friends.

The dream seemed almost true because I thought it was possible. I went to his room after school sometimes with a girlfriend, Kathe, and he and I spoke with each other like friends, as if we were equal, as if he liked me as much as I liked him. We were almost friends that went places together.

I sat with Kathe while she worked on her drawing. Mr. Bayard asked me, "Why aren't you working?" I shrugged my shoulders and smiled. Mr. Bayard shook his head and said, "Just a lazy bum -- stead," and we laughed. He had almost said, "Well, ready to go down to the A&W?" or "Saturday I'm going hiking, want to come?"

Mr. Bayard was real. I thought we were almost friends, and the only reason we weren't was that we hadn't gotten there yet.

The Dream Time

-Four-

It was June. The last day of school had come and the girls could wear pants. I wore jeans and felt like running and jumping. In Art I put my hands behind my head as we sat and called for our pictures when Mr. Bayard held them up. My elbows stuck out jauntily and I watched Mr. Bayard, smiling. He looked at me curiously.

The other girls and I were talking and signing yearbooks. I was sorry I hadn't bought one, because I wouldn't have pictures of my teachers to look at over the summer, remembering. I saw Mr. Bayard walking toward our table. He looked at me, with his sad smile, and handed me his yearbook.

He asked, "Will you sign my yearbook?" and then added to the others, "All of you?"

I bent over the book thoughtfully.

I heard Lisa ask him, "Well, will we see you next

year?"

Mr. Bayard replied, "No, I'm moving to Costa Mesa."

A cold wave drowned with a roar my heart. Mr. Bayard!

School was over. Next year we would be sophomores, then juniors, then seniors, then we would go to college and become teachers ourselves, perhaps. Our whole lives seemed to stretch from this last day forward, through years and over and over, until memories fell like rain. I said the song *Scarborough Fair* would remind me of Miss Loch and *Wonderlove* would cause me to think of Mr. Bayard. We connected our memories with things that lasted, so that one day, years from that final day, we could catch it back. When we caught it, as it threaded through the music, we felt the memories building up and spreading like a fire set by the dream-maker. The dreams returned and with them the living and finally, a far away black star of loneliness. It was the kind of loneliness that made us curl up in the night and cry for the beauty of living.

Jan and I, in our jeans, went to the English class after school was out. Jan wanted Miss Loch to sign her yearbook. The room was full of milling students, hanging on until the last minute. Miss Loch called out, "Anyone who wants, please come sign my yearbook." She glanced at me. I smiled shyly, and she smiled back. But I was too timid to enter the crowd around her book.

I thought about what I had written to Mr. Bayard. The day before, after school, he had asked me if I thought he had taught me anything. He didn't feel like he had taught anything to anyone. I smiled at him then, thinking. Today I had written in his yearbook, "Thank you for teaching me a lot about teaching! Debbie Bumstead." It didn't mean anything.

The Dream Time

I know I should have written -- I wanted to write, "I love you. Debbie Bumstead."
Now it is too late.

Debbie Bumstead

Teen-Age Musings

I could open my curtain here at my work table and look out the window, but I think it is dark out and all I would see is my reflection. What has made this day special to me I can not figure out but I have this "up" feeling like fabulous things happened.

**

I see sluggish ants crawling up the step and soft yellow weeds waving their tips in the sun. Being so close here to the earth I can smell it. The smell is like rain and trees and growing and it is like a piece of the sun cooled and crumbled. I would like some perfume that smells like that and I would put it behind my ears and a touch on my belly button and then all the day I would go about smelling like streets after it rains.

Debbie Bumstead

**

Aren't words wonderful things? I like the ocean, the earth, dragon, child, wild, cracker, and Czechoslovakia. I like the way my German teacher says "Debbie," and I like the way poetry flows through your lips. I don't like bloat, coagulate, and hate. I like words and I like to write.

**

This Sunday in the morning, I was lying there in bed and I was thinking just about silly things like ponies and puppies, milk and cookies and the Sunday funnies. Then, suddenly, I flopped in my bed like a fish and smiled, just smiled right out in mid-air because it is Christmas time.

**

You know, I would like to be a eucalyptus tree leaf. I would have a pretty nice life. On and on I would go, up and down I think I would go and I would feel sticky on the inside and flat on the outside. There is that tree that would belong in me. Trees with leaves, leaves with trees. In every leaf is there a tree? If I were a leaf I think there would be a tree, there in me, with a gnarly old trunk and then leaves again only smaller and tinier than me, right there inside me. I think there would be soft dark dirt in me, too, smelling like hard bugs and rain.

**

The Dream Time

I want to, I want someone to go with me and to look with me at I do not know what. I can't say, I think that I don't know something that I should know. It could be something there in my mind but I just don't see how to let it come to me. And without whatever it is I think my thoughts are like empty boxes waiting to be filled. Maybe I will always feel this, it might be what keeps me wanting to learn some things and to write and to keep trying to think.

My fingers look to me like thoughts and little ideas stretching out and growing. I feel like there is so much likeness and friendship between my hands and my mind that they seem each to live by the other.

The night is here and soon I should go to sleep. I want to write though, it goes through me, this feeling, like a quiet little waterfall that wants me to write. I write for the night, tonight, and for dark green grass that might grow by the waterfall. You can hear the water fall like flowers falling. The grass must smell good like my dreams and I am sleepy now, my mind wants to rest for awhile.

**

If I could turn in my desk here and bend over like I was going to tie my shoes, but instead just keep going, turning into a little mass of me with my arms and legs rolled into my body, I would feel like a blop of clay, I think, and Mr. Reed would come along and see this oval-shaped thing sitting on the seat of this desk. Maybe he would push it off onto the floor and I would land there with a little "thumpsh." Then as everyone started staring at me, I would come undone, shooting my arms out and uncurling my legs like a flower.

41

Debbie Bumstead

I would unfold there on the linoleum and I feel like I would be new-looking like a baby bird. I think I would have a ferocious appetite. All those people in the class - I would see them and I would open my mouth and swallow them all. Down they would go into me, but they would just make me more hungry. Wow, would I be hungry! I would get up and eat the whole room. I wouldn't get big or fat; I would just eat, eat, eat. After I ate the classroom I would eat the whole school and everyone in it, too. I don't know where it would all end. Maybe I would eat the whole universe.

**

Thursday, April 13, 1972 (in German class)

I have an urge to write. What shall I write then? Something. I'm in my German class with not that much to occupy myself with. It is a windy day today and cold. It makes my eyes feel big and dark and cold with dark lashes blowing against my eyelids. Also this weather makes me feel small and rapid like little black alley cats hiding behind garbage cans. And I want to leave this classroom. I want to go hiking down into a grassy valley I know in the hills. There is a large juniper tree and a rock that is most comfortable to sit against.

You can think there. I can sit and think the clearest thoughts. When I am thinking my mind is like a pool that is very clear with all the rocks and mud settled on the bottom in their own patterns. I look at the grass and reeds and rocks around me and I can think, I really can. But when I am here in school many things come into my brain and bother it like someone took a stick and stirred the mud and gravel around to muddle my pool.

The Dream Time

**

I don't even *feel* like writing. The dumb chest of drawers I am staring at makes me so mad. The stupid drawers won't shut right so that one side slants up and the other side flops down. You probably do not even understand - I don't care whether you do or not. What a dumb mood. STUPID, DUMB, IDIOTIC. I feel like I never want to go anywhere; I do not want to grow up; I do not want to do anything. I feel like I would like to be dead.

**

Feeling crummy, crummy, crummy

Oh, I want to scribble all over this paper I want to burst open my whole body because there is something in there that has been bugging the heck out of me all this crappy day. Darn, darn, darn. I know these nights that come after a day like today; I lie in bed and I can't think anything because what I want to think isn't there and I move and toss and my legs go like I'm riding a dumb bicycle and I never can go to sleep. All my insides are crinking around each other because I am so mad at my stupid brain. It needs to be wrung out like a dishrag. It feels like a dead rock. Oh, blah I give it all up.

**

I was walking, just to be walking, yesterday in the very late afternoon. This time, I think, is my favorite time of everyday, when the sun is so low on the horizon that even the short little blades of grass have flickers of shine on them. As

43

Debbie Bumstead

I walked across a lawn, pointed grass shadows were on my bare feet and I thought that the grass blades seem more friendly and human when I know that they also have shadows. I walked down the alley and I heard people in their back yards sitting outside to enjoy the cool. I did not see them often because of fences but their voices drifted to me like a strange kind of air that had noises and sounds to it. All the air seemed to me to like me, it did not make me shiver or sweat, we were equal, it seemed, and I felt that this is the way, almost, that I would want everyday to be like.

This time is also the cats' favorite time of day, I think. I sat down in the alley by our fence and watched the cats wander around; I wiggled sticks for them to play with and I made up names for the ugly strays that are here one day and then I never see them again. I doubt if it made them feel any better, that a human being had thought enough of them to name them. If I were sick and starving, between a name and food, I would surely pick food.

The sun was almost gone and I heard my family talking, through the screen door, about cookies and milk. That sounded good and I thought perhaps we would have an interesting topic for discussion tonight so I was ready to go in. But still I sat there in the darkness and I felt that this certainly has been a good kind of day and I wished that other people might be having the same feeling I was then. I thought of my friends and everyone that I did not even know who might be taking a moment to just think. It seems like a lot of people are so busy they do not think, but how would I know? I cannot know their thoughts. I went in then, because it was cold now and the cold seemed to be making that nice feeling shiver away.

The Dream Time

**

The wind is blowing against my body, pressing against me, it makes me feel like I am really really here. It is night, the hill I stand on is wild, and a white cat wandering passes by me. Things are not the same. It is just a feeling I am having.

**

What would it be like to have feet at the end of your arms and hands at the end of your legs? I would walk around on my hands and wave my arms and wiggle my toes in the air and then when I met an old friend I would shake feet with him. How would I play tennis? I guess I would look rather strange running around on my hands and having a tennis racquet grasped at the end of one of my feet.

**

When Mr. Clark twanged a pink card to the person who owned it, it flitted over my way, I caught it neatly between my teeth, nonchalantly took it in my hand and politely gave it to the owner. The class gasped in amazement at my skill but I simply looked out the window. It was nothing to me.

**

I was walking to the P.E. room yesterday, looking out of my eyes at the sight before me, the trees and houses in the distance, the locker room, and the girls walking to and fro. The air was cool and clean in my eyes and I thought, "It seems to me that when I look out at the world and see everything fresh and clear, I feel like I ought to look that way myself. I feel like I ought to look fresh and clear because when I see out my eyes that which I see is a part of me. But when I look in the mirror I don't seem right; it doesn't look like my face fits with the rest of the world and me. My face doesn't fit what I see out of it.

**

Magic....

It is a very light night outside. The alley is quiet and still and the white of the houses and garages seems like a sort of fluorescent gray. Some of the trees around are already bare of their leaves and they make India ink sketches against the clouds, others still losing leaves are extra quiet tonight and motionless. It is surely a time for magic. Straight over and above there is an opening in the clouds; in all the heavens there is only this one opening and at this precise magic moment the moon moves into it, leaving thin clouds wisping after. This is magic.

And nearby in a bush a startled sparrow gives a little shriek and struggles flapping through the bush and out and away into the air. In this one second event the night is frightened and the magic runs away. The house seems like a better place to be now, warm and protecting from bad omens.

The Dream Time

About the Author
Debbie Bumstead lives in Reno, Nevada with her family of
humans and animals. Debbie is also the illustrator of the
Smileytooth series of dental hygiene books.

Made in the USA
Charleston, SC
12 November 2012